Reports, Proposals, and Procedures

A WRITE IT WELL GUIDE

by Natasha Terk

A self-paced training program

Write It Well
Business writing that gets results.

Corporations, professional associations, and other organizations may be eligible for special discounts on bulk quantities of Write It Well books and training courses. For more information, call (510) 868-3322, or email us at info@writeitwell.com.

Publisher: Write It Well
                    PO Box 13098
                    Oakland, CA 94661

                    (510) 868-3322

                    info@writeitwell.com
                    writeitwell.com

Author: Natasha Terk

Editor: Christopher Disman

To order this book, visit our website, writeitwell.com.

Our publications include the following books, e-books, and e-learning modules from The Write It Well Series on Business Writing:

Professional Writing Skills

Effective Email: Concise, Clear Writing to Advance Your Business Needs

Land the Job: Writing Effective Resumes and Cover Letters

Develop and Deliver Effective Presentations

Writing Performance Reviews

Write It Well offers a variety of customized on-site and online training courses, including the following:

Effective Email

Professional Writing Skills

Writing Performance Reviews

Writing Resumes and Cover Letters

Technical Writing

Marketing and Social Media Writing

Management Communication Skills

Global Teamwork and Meeting Skills

Presentation Skills

Train-the-trainer kits are also available to accompany these courses.

We offer coaching to improve individual professionals' writing and presenting skills. We also offer editorial, layout, and writing services to help individual authors and teams send out well-organized documents in language that's correct, clear, concise, and engaging.

For more information about any of our content or services,

- Visit writeitwell.com
- Email us at info@writeitwell.com
- Or give us a call at (510) 655-6477

CONTENTS

INTRODUCTION

Many people in business need to write long, multisection documents to pass on detailed information or propose a course of action. For instance, you can use long documents for these purposes:

- To describe the steps of a procedure

- To present the results of a research study

- To describe the uses of a line of products

- To explain the likely benefits of a potential project

- To pitch your professional services

- To provide facts to support a request

For any multisection business document, logical organization is necessary to help people see a structure behind the details. Clear writing is necessary so that your readers will understand each point you make. Concise writing is also necessary to show respect for your readers' time and sustained attention. Long-winded, confusing, disorganized passages can turn any long document into a chore for any reader.

Here are some obstacles to writing clearly and concisely in a multisection document:

- You may have so much information that it's hard to know several things:
    - How to organize your ideas
    - How to decide which ideas you'll lead with
    - How to decide which ideas to include or leave out

- You may have many readers. Different readers may have different needs for information and different levels of knowledge about your subject.

- Several people may be involved in the writing process, and contrasts between their writing styles can distract your readers. Substantial editing may be necessary to give the document a coherent voice.

This course offers a step-by-step planning process to help you address all these challenges.

This course will prepare you to take several actions toward a clear, concise, well-organized multisection document:

- Break the ice to start outlining your document's sections

- Identify what kinds of guidance your readers will need to follow your points and find details quickly

- Decide when to include information, leave it out, or place it in an attachment or appendix

- Work as a team to fill out a shared outline and write with a unified, dynamic voice

This course also offers tools toward **your professional development.** The writing tasks above will help you communicate more effectively as a team member or team leader. See the sidebars on pages 6, 10, 22, 24, and 42 for ways to consciously link your written communication skills with your leadership, teamwork, project management, problem-solving, analytical, and other core professional abilities. Also see other books in The Write It Well Series on Business Writing (e.g., *Develop and Deliver Effective Presentations*) for further professional-development suggestions.

Step-by-step guide to the course

The steps in the following four lessons will help you master the challenges of writing multisection professional documents.

Lesson 1: Outline a long document

- Identify your readers' needs, interests, and concerns

- Identify your business needs

- Identify and answer readers' single most important question

- Identify readers' other key questions

Lesson 2: Develop your outline

- Group related questions, and then answer them

- Write summary statements

- Write section headings and subheadings

Lesson 3: Draft your document

- Follow section outlines to begin writing
- Develop useful lists, charts, and visuals
- Draft an introduction
- Draft a document summary
- Compose key sentences that express your most important messages

Lesson 4: Use dynamic language

- Use concise language
- Use active language
- Write problem-action-result (PAR) stories
- Use plain English

Some premises for style and content

This course is based on the following premises for the **STYLE GOALS** that all professional documents should try to meet:

- Grammar, punctuation, and spelling are correct
- Sentences and paragraphs are short enough to grasp easily
- The writers choose language that their readers will be able to follow easily

See Write It Well's book *Professional Writing Skills* for further techniques to meet these standards — in business documents of any length and any level of complexity.

In addition to the style goals above, this course is based on the following premises for the **CONTENT GOALS** that all professional documents should try to meet:

- The writers clearly formulate their most important point and lead the document with it

- The writers clearly formulate each section's most important point and lead the section with it

- Headings and subheadings provide a helpful road map through the document

- A report or proposal summarizes complex information before launching into details

- A procedure clearly separates process steps and presents them in chronological order

Some definitions

We use the word *report* broadly, to refer to a professional document that the writers use primarily to pass on information. We use the word *proposal* to refer to a document that the writers use primarily to explain their professional abilities and to suggest that clients or customers engage in a transaction.

We use the word *procedure* to refer to a document that presents a series of steps that will lead readers to accomplish a specific objective. Reports are primarily informative, while procedures are primarily persuasive. Proposals blend informative and persuasive approaches.

Lesson 1 includes guidelines for deciding whether your next long, multisection document has a primarily informative or primarily persuasive business purpose. The first three lessons of the book all conclude with document-outlining activities that you'll find directly relevant to your work:

- **PAGE 20** includes an activity to outline a report

- **PAGE 34** includes an activity to outline a related proposal

- **PAGE 70** includes an activity to outline a related procedure

1 OUTLINE A LONG DOCUMENT

OVERVIEW

This lesson features a step-by-step process to outline a long, multisection document — preparing you to take these actions:

- Assess your readers' needs, interests, and concerns

- Identify what business need your document will advance

- Identify the single most important question your document will answer

- Summarize this question's answer in one to three sentences

- Identify readers' other key questions and turn them into the topics for the sections of your document

The chapter uses two types of long document — requests for proposals (RFPs) as well as reports — to illustrate these outlining techniques.

Step 1: Identify your readers' needs, interests, and concerns

Begin the outlining process by looking at the subject from your readers' point of view. Your readers may have different backgrounds, interests, needs, concerns, and levels of technical knowledge.

Consider what your readers already know about your topic, and what they need to learn. Also consider their levels of interest, how they'll use the information, and whether you need to persuade them to take action.

Some readers are familiar with your subject, and they won't need you to establish much context. Some readers are not familiar with your subject, and they'll need you to explain concepts in clear, plain English. Other readers may object to your ideas, and these readers will need you to offer persuasive reasons for accepting what you suggest.

Most long, multisection business documents have more than one type of reader:

- **PRIMARY READERS** often make decisions based on what they read

- **SECONDARY READERS** may only read part of the document, they may need you to establish more context to explain your ideas, and they may have less interest in the topic than your primary readers

When you plan a long document, think about previous interactions you've had with your primary and secondary readers. Keep these two groups of readers in mind as you read the questions on the next page.

Show leadership by understanding your audience

Identifying other people's interests and needs can translate into long-term benefits for your career — for instance, by strengthening your leadership skills. Analyzing your readers' or listeners' needs always makes you a more effective business communicator:

- Understanding different people's interests can help you motivate your colleagues or team members in an email, a conversation, or a meeting
- This process can prepare you to coach or mentor colleagues when they need to learn new information and you need to share your professional expertise
- And the process can help you plan and lead effective presentations, as you identify what a specific audience wants and needs to hear

Consider all the questions below *before* you start to write. Below you'll see some questions to answer when your writing has a persuasive component. These first three sets of questions are helpful when your primary purpose is to **PASS ON INFORMATION TO YOUR READERS.**

- **WHAT DO YOUR READERS ALREADY KNOW ABOUT THE TOPIC?** You need to know how much readers already know before you can determine what they'll need to learn from the document. For example, primary readers may already be familiar with the situation, while secondary readers are not. In that case, you should include some context in an introduction, attachment, cover letter, or appendix so that secondary readers can follow along.

- **HOW WILL YOUR READERS USE THE IDEAS?** This question should affect the level of detail in the document. For example, primary readers may use your ideas to implement phase two of a project plan; these readers will therefore need more details than a group of secondary readers who merely want an overview of the project status. Ask yourself these kinds of questions:

    - Will readers decide whether to take action and decide what action to take?

    - Will they determine whether something was done or will be done correctly?

    - Should they increase their general knowledge about a project or a situation?

    - Will all readers use the information the same way?

- **IF YOU'RE WRITING ABOUT A TECHNICAL SUBJECT, WHAT ARE YOUR DIFFERENT READERS' LEVELS OF TECHNICAL KNOWLEDGE?** Will readers understand the terms and concepts that you use to discuss this subject with expert colleagues? Will readers need you to use everyday language instead? If so, you may need to compile a glossary or draft an additional summary in plain English.

The next three sets of questions are especially helpful when your primary purpose is **TO PER-SUADE YOUR READERS TO TAKE ACTION.**

- **IS THERE A PERSUASIVE COMPONENT TO WHAT YOU'RE WRITING?** Do you want to influence readers in some way, or sell them on some line of action? If so, what are the benefits for readers? Are they ready to say yes? Likely to say no? Undecided? What objections or concerns are they likely to have?

- **HOW INTERESTED ARE READERS IN YOUR SUBJECT?** Are they already interested, or are you hoping that the document will build interest?

- **WHAT OTHER POINTS ABOUT READERS ARE IMPORTANT TO CONSIDER FOR THIS DOCUMENT?** Is the information critical for any readers? Are any readers in a hurry for the information? Is the information you're presenting likely to surprise readers? Could some readers be uncomfortable with your ideas?

The more of these questions you can answer about your readers, the easier it will be to outline your document to accomplish two crucial tasks:

- To meet *readers'* needs to see clear, concise, well-organized writing

And to advance *your* professional needsThe more of these questions you can answer about your readers, the easier it will be to outline your document to accomplish two crucial tasks:

- To meet *readers'* needs to see clear, concise, well-organized writing

- And to advance *your* professional needs

TRY IT:

Think of a long document that you need to write for work. Use the space below to identify your reader's likely needs, interests, and concerns.

Plan how you'll write to mystery readers

What if all or some of your readers are people you've never met or spoken with? If you're able to respectfully ask them any of the questions on the preceding page, then ask away. If direct questions aren't possible or don't seem like a good idea, then some educated guesses can help you frame a long document for readers whose needs are a mystery.

First, consider what you do know about the readers — or what you can safely assume. Suppose that you're proposing a marketing plan for a midsize company, and its primary reader will be the company president. She's the one who'll decide whether to accept, modify, or reject your plan.

Imagine you've never spoken with the president because she travels frequently, and you've been dealing with the head of the marketing team. But you can make some assumptions about the president's likely needs as a reader. She's likely to be busy; to be concerned about the time, costs, and resources that your marketing plan will consume; and to be interested in how your plan will benefit the company.

Next, consider what you don't know. For example, you might have to guess or ask about the president's level of knowledge about marketing, as well as what she already knows about this kind of project.

This kind of thinking helps you communicate more effectively by transforming strangers into readers who have needs, interests, and concerns that you appreciate.

Step 2: Identify your business needs

The key to writing a successful long document is to keep your readers' point of view in mind throughout the writing process. After you've completed Step 1, also step back and think clearly about why you're planning a document for this particular set of readers. Namely, what specific business need does your document represent?

Articulating this purpose helps you think clearly about your readers' questions and also map out answers that will advance your specific goal in writing. Most business documents have just one of two primary purposes: to inform readers, or to persuade them to take action:

- The primary purpose of a **REPORT** is usually to pass on <u>information</u>.

- The primary purpose of a **PROPOSAL** is usually to <u>persuade</u> clients or customers to engage in a business transaction, based on relevant information.

- A **PROCEDURE** presents <u>information</u> through a series of steps, in a <u>persuasive</u> way. Readers should understand what specific steps they should take to accomplish a stated objective.

In other words, reports are primarily informative, procedures are primarily persuasive, and proposals blend informative and persuasive approaches in different sections.

Identify your professional needs for each document you write

Writing is often critical for professional teamwork, and team members and leaders communicate more effectively when they identify a primary purpose for *every* document they write — e.g., a quick email, a midway status report, or a presentation of findings for a journal. **TEAM LEADERS** often need to communicate a clear vision in writing — e.g.,

- To give team members precise information
- To persuade them of the importance of an activity
- Or to pass on clear instructions

TEAM MEMBERS also need to have a clear grasp on the purpose of their emails and reports. A team often works more effectively when its members use writing to highlight a shared purpose — e.g.,

- By explaining they need further information
- By providing clear, informative progress updates
- Or by persuasively suggesting possible courses of action

Consciously identifying your purpose and your business needs can benefit all of the long and short professional documents you write.

The journalistic triangle

Have you ever noticed that the first paragraphs of many news articles contain the most important information? The rest of the article then provides further details that support, explain, expand on, or illustrate that information.

News editors know that readers often scan only the headline and first part of an article. They also know that the final paragraphs of a piece may be cut out or put on a separate webpages. That's why editors often answer readers' most important question right at the beginning, as shown in the example below.

Keep this triangle in mind when you write. You meet two goals when you put the most important information first: you answer the readers' most important question right away, and you provide readers with a context for details that will follow.

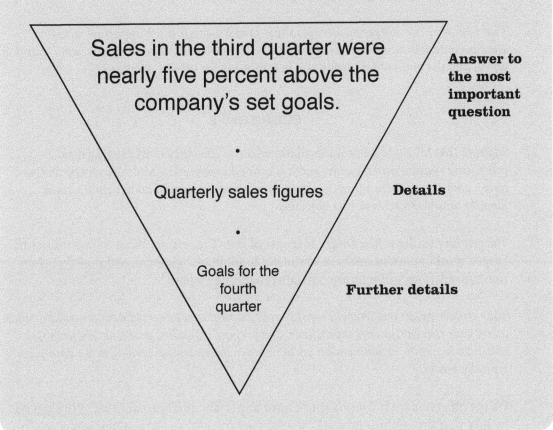

Step 3: Identify and answer
readers' single most important question

Your document should lead with the information that your reader will find most relevant, so your next step is to identify your readers' single most important question. Then you'll compose a statement, in one to three sentences, that summarizes the answer. Here are two scenarios, single questions, and answering statements that are each one or two sentences long.

SCENARIO 1

Your readers' most important question might be, <u>"What steps can we take to reduce operating costs during the coming fiscal year?"</u> Your answer might be, *"We analyzed your operations and found that three measures will help you reduce costs. We recommend consolidating two staff positions, purchasing tablet computers for field representatives, and reducing the number of off-site meetings."*

That two-sentence statement answers these readers' single most important question. Details could follow in separate document sections — *which* two positions, *what* brand of tablet, and the *optimal* frequency and *best* location for off-site meetings.

SCENARIO 2

Suppose that Midstate Bank wants to improve the efficiency of its existing data processing system, which is slow and has limited capabilities. Midstate representatives have asked you to write a proposal describing what you would do to help the bank identify options to achieve that objective.

The primary reader is Jose Diego, Manager of Data Processing. What do you think Mr. Diego's most important question would be? It might be, <u>"How can we know that your recommendations will improve our data processing system?"</u>

Your answer might be, *"We will identify your current and projected data processing needs, assess your current system's capabilities, and prepare a detailed proposal. The proposal will include specific recommendations to improve the system, according to the data you typically process."*

On the other hand, Mr. Diego's single most important question could be, <u>"Why should we hire your firm for this project?"</u> Your answer might then be the single sentence, *"We have the experience and qualifications to help you achieve your objectives, we understand what work you need done, and our prices are competitive."*

TRY IT:
· · · · · · ·

Think of a long document you need to write for work. Use the space below to identify and answer your reader's single most important question.

Pitch your services in a proposal
· ·

Many businesspeople feel tongue-tied when we need to explain the benefits of our professional services. This kind of explanation can be crucial for a successful proposal.

Pages 85–86 include a formula to make this process straightforward: **problem-action-result (PAR) stories.**

Step 4: Identify readers' other key questions

So far, you've answered questions about your readers' needs and identified the single most important question your document will answer. You're ready now to identify the major topics the document will address.

Think about the subject from your readers' point of view and then write down all the questions that your readers are likely to have. This is a brainstorming process. Don't stop to evaluate or organize questions as you write them down: you'll do that later.

This process has several advantages:

- By starting with readers' questions (instead of the answers that you already have), you focus on the information readers need.

- You may have worked very hard to gather information, but it's risky to confuse the value of your hard work with the value the information will have for your readers. Carefully considering readers' needs is the best way to make sure your information will engage them and add up to a useful document.

- As you'll see below, the readers' questions will help you determine what information to include and how to organize your document into sections. In Lesson 2, you'll see how to build on this process to fill out your document's outline.

On the next few pages, we illustrate this outlining step by identifying readers' key questions for one kind of business document: requests for proposals (RFPs).

Brainstorming guidelines

The purpose of brainstorming is to free yourself to come up with as many ideas, questions, and answers as possible. You can do so only if you allow yourself to generate ideas without stopping the flow by censoring or evaluating them.

Begin with a question such as, "Why should my reader do what I want?" or, "What does my reader need to know about this topic?"

Write down every point that comes to mind without censoring, evaluating, or organizing the points. Don't worry about whether a point is meaningful or even whether you've already listed it. Just keep listing. You'll eliminate unnecessary or redundant points later.

Keep going until you believe you've written down all the important points. You may get stuck. If so, then take a walk, tackle another task, or talk the situation over with a colleague. Then return to the brainstorming process.

Focus again on the beginning question. Read your list out loud, and add any additional points that come to mind.

TRY IT:

Think of a multisection document you need to write for work. Use the space on these two pages to identify and answer your reader's key questions about your topic.

Write an RFP in six question-and-answer stages

The task of *writing* an RFP is actually very similar to the task of *responding to* an RFP: you build your outline by answering your readers' questions.

Vendors who assemble a proposal should put themselves in the shoes of the people who requested that proposal through an RFP. In a very similar way, people who write an RFP should put themselves in the shoes of the vendors who'll respond by sending in proposals. Both groups need to complete Step 4 of this chapter by identifying their readers' key questions.

Here's a six-stage procedure (Stages A–F) to write a solid RFP. (If you get stuck *responding* to an RFP, you can also try to use these steps to put yourself in the shoes of the people who wrote it and then outline a document based on the readers' key questions.)

A. FIGURE OUT WHAT YOUR ORGANIZATION NEEDS.

1. Identify the scope of the services your organization needs, or the features of the products you need. Think about what you *must* have, and also what might be nice to have if a potential vendor can provide that, too.

2. Identify a practical way potential vendors could satisfy your real need, and identify who is likely to have this ability. The main vendor question you need to answer is, "How can we help you?"

Again, you're more likely to get the responses you want when you clearly describe what you need, how the respondent can satisfy the need, and what minimum qualifications you expect all respondents to have.

B. WRITE A COVER LETTER THAT PROVIDES AN OVERVIEW OF THE RFP THAT FOLLOWS. THINK ABOUT TWO AUDIENCES.

1. Readers' main question here is, "Is this RFP really addressed to me?" Respondents who clearly would *not* be a good fit should recognize from your cover letter that they couldn't satisfy your requirements. State all your minimum requirements and deal-breakers up front. If you only want to read proposals from local businesses, then no out-of-state people should waste their time by reading past your RFP's cover letter.

2. Respondents who *would* be a good fit should get a clear overview from the cover letter of what you want to buy, and what your timeframe is. Make sure the cover letter includes a concise statement of what you need (you can unpack the details in later sections). The cover letter should also state the receive-by date for proposals, and the timeframe for the winning vendor's deliverables.

C. PROVIDE A CLEAR STRUCTURE SO THAT RESPONDENTS CAN UNDERSTAND WHAT THEY SHOULD OFFER.

1. The main vendor question here is, <u>"What kind of offers do you want to read?"</u> Introduce your organization in one section, moving from general information to details that help respondents understand how this specific, proposed project will benefit you.

2. Set out the scope of services or required product in another section. Distinguish between your requirements and your preferences. You don't have to explain exactly how you'll rate proposals or decide on a winning vendor (although it's helpful if you do). But you should give respondents a strong sense of how good a fit they are for your project.

D. TELL THE RESPONDENTS WHAT TO INCLUDE IN THEIR PROPOSALS, AND WHAT TO EXPECT AFTER THEY SUBMIT IT.

1. The main vendor question here is, <u>"What should I include in my proposal?"</u> Use headings and section breaks to give respondents a structured outline for the proposals they'll write:

    *   In separate sections, they should send you clear overviews of their organizations, the qualifications of key personnel, the product or services they'll provide, and their proposed budgets and timelines.

    *   This uniform outline will help you sift through all the proposals you get and then select the best one. If any respondents fail to follow your outline, that failure may suggest that they won't understand or provide what your organization needs.

2. Finally, give respondents a timeline for your reply to their proposals. The vendor question here is, <u>"When will I hear back from you?"</u> Say when you anticipate determining the winning vendor, and say what the next steps will be for your organization and theirs.

E. REVIEW THE PROPOSALS YOU RECEIVE, AND DECIDE WHO'LL SELL YOU THE PRODUCTS OR SERVICES YOU NEED.

Clear writing pays off for everyone in **this reading stage of the process.** Respondents have already benefitted because you gave them precise instructions on what kind of proposal they should send you. And you now benefit from reading proposals that relate directly to the specific needs you clearly spelled out in your RFP.

F. COMMUNICATE WITH ALL BIDDERS AFTER YOU DECIDE WHICH PROPOSAL WAS BEST.

1. One likely question for losing vendors is, <u>"Did my proposal fall short?"</u> Bidders that didn't win your business deserve a letter. Give them information about where they fell short — e.g., by not addressing a question sufficiently, or scoring lower than others on a point system.

2. The main question winning vendors will have is, <u>"What can I keep doing right?"</u> Tell the winning bidder precisely why they won your business. Explaining what aspect of their proposal won you over may help them deliver exactly the products or services you're looking for.

Clear writing in Stage F above helps all RFP respondents understand their proposals' strengths and weaknesses. That clear understanding may pave the way for good future relations between their organization and yours. All these RFP/proposal questions and answers can provide a reliable framework for good business relations.

TRY IT

· · · · · ·

Here's an excerpt from an RFP. Put yourself in the shoes of either the people who *wrote* the RFP or the people who'll *respond* to it — whichever group is a better match for your own professional writing needs.

Using your computer or some notepaper, list all the questions you can find in this excerpt:

> We are requesting that you provide us with references and where possible, samples of similar training programs that your company has developed. We would then request that you provide us with a rate and a time commitment to develop the first three modules of the training program described on the following pages. We would also request that you provide us with a description of the way in which you would approach this project, as well as the names and qualifications of the people who would do the actual development work. We are looking for a company that can demonstrate stability since we envision that this will be a long-term relationship.

ANSWERS

· · · · · · · · ·

Here are some explicit and implied questions you might have identified:

- Are you able to provide references? From whom?

- What similar programs have you developed? If you haven't developed similar programs, then why are you confident that you can develop one for us?

- What will you charge to develop the first three modules?

- How long will it take you to develop these modules?

- What steps would you follow to complete the project?

- Who would undertake the development work? What are their qualifications?

- How do we know your company is stable enough for a long-term relationship? Do you want to commit to working with us in the long term?

ACTIVITY:
A MILLION-DOLLAR REPORT

. . . .

You're ready to draw on this lesson's outlining techniques to begin the outline of a report. Start by imagining that your organization is likely to make a perfect resource available to you or your department.

But also imagine that a few important decision makers need to see **A WELL-ORGANIZED REPORT** from you, first, that describes the current state of your department. Follow these three steps to outline the report.

1. Use your imagination to visualize this perfect resource — picturing something wonderful but relatively plausible. You might visualize a fleet of minivans or state-of-the-art technology, or a thousand dollars, one million dollars, or more.

2. Use the space below to outline a report on the way things currently are in your department — focusing on whatever aspects of your work matter most to you. Settle on two or more departmental activities that you might discuss in separate report sections.

3. The next chapter will give you a chance to expand this **REPORT** outline into a **PROPOSAL** for you to receive this perfect resource and put it to good use. For now, however, assume that your reader's questions relate to how things *are*, and not to how they *could be* if you obtained the new resource. Assume that readers would see any speculation about improvements as unwelcome clutter in your report.

2 DEVELOP YOUR OUTLINE

OVERVIEW

In Lesson 1, you learned a process to outline your document. The outline shows the preliminary headings for the various document sections along with some of the readers' key questions for each section.

Lesson 2 provides a similar step-by-step process. In this lesson, you'll learn to identify the information to include in each section and subsection of your document. The process will seem familiar because it's also based on identifying readers' questions.

In fact, you should think of each section as a mini-document with its own clear internal logic. You follow the same basic steps to develop the outline for each section that you follow to develop the outline for your document as a whole.

This lesson will prepare you to take these actions:

- Group related questions and answer them
- Write summary statements
- Write section headings

Step 1: Group related questions and answer them

In this step, you'll begin to develop the content for your document by answering the questions you've already posed. This process develops and expands the outline for your document's main sections and subsections.

Use your questions and answers to expand your outline for one document section, following this five-step process:

A. **Review the list of questions you've identified.**

B. **Group related questions together,** dividing them under two or more themes.

C. **Delete any unnecessary or redundant questions,** applying these two criteria:

- Does this question help readers grasp the document's central topic?

- Does this question advance my business needs?

D. **Briefly answer the overall questions, adding details as items in a list format.** If the answer to a question is lengthy or you don't have all the details, try one of these two processes to sketch out information that the answer will include:

- Use a numbered list if the items follow chronological order or a similar logic.

- Assemble the items in a bulleted list if you can fit them under a single heading but could also rearrange them without changing the logic.

Delete information as a form of problem solving

In Step C above, it can feel painful to apply the words *redundant* and *unnecessary* to ideas that are valuable to you. But this analytical selection process represents **PROBLEM SOLVING,** a core professional ability. A frequent business problem is deciding whether an idea is relevant, off topic, or not important enough to include in your current message — spoken or written.

Successful professional communication is often the result of problem solving — from deciding what details do and don't belong in a report, to mapping out a focused presentation agenda, to deciding just how much to say in a high-stakes email. Business readers rarely have time to spare, and overcrowding your message will waste their time. That's a significant problem.

You'll successfully solve many communication challenges by identifying which ideas belong in your message, omitting the rest, and moving on. Respecting your listeners' time will boost their trust in you as a professional who's worth listening to.

E. **ARRANGE THESE QUESTION/ANSWER SETS IN WHATEVER ORDER SEEMS MOST LOGICAL TO YOU.** Test your logic by asking yourself if this new sequence of ideas will accomplish two things: answering your readers' questions while also advancing your business needs.

Arrange each set of questions in a list, and give each list an introductory statement that establishes a common factor for all the questions it contains. Grouping questions into lists has these three advantages:

- A list makes it easy to identify a unifying theme as well as the details that fall under that theme.

- A list makes it easy to organize information so that it has a logical structure.

- The list format can be a tool to focus your writing. If any detail doesn't fit under the unifying theme for your new introductory statement, then that detail becomes either a candidate for a new theme or a candidate for deletion.

TRY IT:

The questions below are for a report section headed "Reasons for Equipping Field Representatives with Tablet Computers." Which questions would you group together? Which redundant or unnecessary questions would you eliminate?

The letters in front of the questions are to help you organize them. Turn to page 25 for one solution to this organization challenge.

SECTION HEADING: Reasons for Equipping Field Representatives with Tablet Computers

A.	How would field reps use the tablet computers?
B.	Would tablets make field reps more productive?
C.	How would our clients benefit if we equip field reps with tablets?
D.	Would tablets save field reps time?
E.	Would giving field reps tablets save us money?
F.	What would tablets let field reps do that they can't do now?
G.	Would having tablets make field reps happier?

Count ideas for an authoritative, user-friendly document

Any business document is likely to seem more impressive when your writing displays **ANALYTICAL SKILLS.** Analysis is a natural part of the planning process. One simple way to include helpful analytical guidance is to count your ideas and then include numbers in your sentences and document formatting.

Numbers can act as a heads-up for information that your readers are about to encounter. For instance, you might begin a bulleted list with the introductory statement, "We see <u>four</u> primary benefits: • • • •." Or you might add a section heading that reads, "<u>FOUR</u> BENEFITS," followed by four paragraphs—one for each benefit as you explain it to your readers.

Quantifying information shows that you thoroughly understand your topic and that you've taken some pains to help your readers understand it, too. It's a considerate way to lead readers through your ideas.

TRY IT: Look through some documents you've written for your job — especially documents that seemed complex at the time. Could simple quantitative analysis have made your writing seem more authoritative and user friendly?

ANSWERS
· · · · · · · · ·

Here's one way to group the questions on page 23; you may have grouped them differently. Some items are moved out of the alphabetical order you saw above, and unnecessary or redundant questions are crossed out. Each overall question leads to a subsection for this report section, so preliminary subsection headings are also added.

Reasons to Equip Field Representatives with Tablet Computers

OVERALL QUESTION: How would field reps use tablet computers?

SUBSECTION HEADING: USES OF TABLETS

A.   How would field reps use tablets?

OVERALL QUESTION: Would tablets make field reps more productive?

SUBSECTION HEADING: INCREASED PRODUCTIVITY

B.   Would tablets make field reps more productive?

[Part C is moved down]

D.   ~~Would tablets save field reps time?~~

F.   What would tablets let field reps do that they can't do now?

G.   ~~Would having tablets make field reps happier?~~

OVERALL QUESTION: How would equipping field reps with tablet computers benefit our clients?

SUBSECTION HEADING: BENEFITS TO CLIENT

C.   How would our clients benefit if we equip field reps with tablets?

OVERALL QUESTION: Would giving field reps tablets save us money?

SUBSECTION HEADING: COST SAVINGS

E.   Would giving field reps tablets save us money?

Project management and well-organized ideas

Grouping your ideas is a helpful process for many professional activities — e.g., **PROJECT MANAGEMENT.** Clear categories of ideas can give you an overview of all the project details you need to track and complete, grouped by deadlines and types of activity.

Grouping your project details into categories can help you manage complexity, stay on schedule, and not lose sight of the forest for the trees. And clear writing is often vital for successful project management — from a detailed project proposal, through countless emails about progress and challenges between team leaders and members, to a final project report.

As you learned earlier, the content for the section of a long document should represent answers to questions. Starting with your readers' questions, instead of your own answers, makes it easier to determine what information to include and to leave out.

You'll answer the questions for each document section after you've combined related questions and eliminated unnecessary questions. Keep in mind that you're not drafting the document yet—you're developing your section outline as preparation for the first draft.

Don't write out the complete answer to each question yet. For now, identify list themes and add just a few words per list item. Just provide yourself with a clear start to each detail that you'll fill in with complete sentences later on.

If you're not sure whether a detail deserves a place in your expanding outline, then return to your two main tasks:

- Answering your reader's questions
- Shaping the document to advance your informative or persuasive business needs

If any detail doesn't seem to fit either purpose, then it's probably best to delete it.

Step 2: Write summary statements

In Lesson 1, you learned to write a statement of one to three sentences that summarizes the answer to your readers' most important question about the document's central topic. These summary statements are like the top part of the journalistic triangle: the statements provide readers with your most important information and prepare readers for the content that follows.

You'll write summary statements for each document section and any subsections. Summary statements are helpful in three main ways:

- They make it much easier to write the first draft

- They provide a context to help readers follow the information in the document

- As you'll see in Lesson 3, these statements also provide the foundation for the document introduction and any executive summary that readers may need

ASK YOURSELF ...

Here's an easy way to develop a summary statement. Ask, "If I had only five seconds to communicate the most essential information about this topic or detail, what would I say?" Then write down the answer.

Pitch your services

Have you ever practiced an elevator pitch — a concise explanation of how your services make you a great professional partner to accomplish one kind of task? Pages 85–86 include a variation on this kind of answer to the question, "What's in it for me if I decide to work with you?" You may need to include this kind of information in a summary statement.

Use summary statements
to inform readers or to establish a theme

There are two types of summary statements. One type directly answers the overall question for the section, topic, or subtopic — summarizing your most important information. The other type of summary statement simply introduces details to come.

TO ANSWER A QUESTION

SECTION HEADING: PLANT OPENING DELAYED UNTIL NOVEMBER

SUMMARY STATEMENT: "Although the original schedule stipulated that the new processing plant would begin operations on September 20, several key pieces of equipment will not be ready until mid-July. We now plan to open the plant on November 1."

TO ESTABLISH A THEME

SECTION HEADING: BENEFITS PACKAGES

SUMMARY STATEMENT: "Below you will find details of each benefits package, including eligibility criteria and enrollment procedures."

TRY IT:
· · · · · · · ·

Below is the content for one section of a report: "RESULTS OF CUSTOMER SURVEY." Write a summary statement that accurately summarizes the section content. Keep in mind that the summary statement should be no longer than three sentences.

RESULTS OF CUSTOMER SURVEY

SECTION CONTENT

- 2500 survey forms sent to customers re: payment preferences

- 1173 responses

- 983 prefer using credit card

- 120 want an invoice & will pay by check

- 372 would use automatic deduction option

- 833 want longer grace period

SUMMARY STATEMENT (Write it in below):

Answers
• • • • • • • • •

Here's one writer's summary statement. Yours may differ.

RESULTS OF CUSTOMER SURVEY

SUMMARY STATEMENT

We received responses from almost 1,200 customers — about half the customers who received surveys. Almost 1,000 customers prefer paying by credit card, and more than 800 would like a longer grace period.

Step 3: Write section headings and subheadings

You've already learned how to write preliminary section headings; now you'll make sure they adequately describe the section content. You'll also learn how to write subheadings.

As you develop your section outlines, you'll expand the overall questions into preliminary section headings and subsection headings. To complete your writing plan, you'll refine those preliminary headings to clearly indicate what details will follow.

Headings and subheadings provide readers with a useful road map that helps them locate information quickly. Headings should tell readers what's ahead and help them focus on key information.

In the example below, notice how much more information readers gain from the second version of each heading.

Version 1	Version 2
Scope of work	Tasks involved in overhauling the health plan
Situation	Problems with the existing health plan
Criteria	Criteria for evaluating health plan options
Options	Comparison of five health plan options

The example below is an outline of the work that design company Paradigm Inc. plans to do for its client Milburn and Associates. Notice that the heading "Corporate Identity" fails to describe what kind of work Paradigm will do. The heading also ignores additional information the section covers, such as the approach the company will use.

ORIGINAL

CORPORATE IDENTITY

We understand that Milburn and Associates plans to develop a new identity, including a new name and new graphics. At the company, you recognize a need for broader public recognition and an image that is appropriate for the 21st century. At Paradigm, we are ready to help with that process.

Milburn and Associates started refining and producing paper in 1990; although you have continued to introduce new products, you have made few changes to your image. As a result of information gleaned from customer surveys and opinions voiced by members of the Board of Directors, management has decided to modify the way the company presents itself to the public.

To begin our search for a new identity for Milburn and Associates, Paradigm will interview six managers responsible for developing, managing, and marketing the company's paper products. We also plan to interview selected customers to attain a more in-depth understanding of your long-term business objectives, target markets, communications channels, desired image, and identity.

We will review any existing research, corporate planning documents, and statements of corporate objectives that might help us understand your identity needs. While we do not need exhaustive information, we do want a clear understanding of major corporate issues and directions. We will also review any names you have previously developed and considered.

Based on the results of the interviews and research, our team will prepare a short list of finalist names. Criteria for selecting names will include how effectively the names meet the communication objectives, how memorable the names are, whether they are easy to pronounce, their graphics potential, and their potential advertising impact.

The design team will then investigate design concepts for each of the name candidates. This design step will show the potential for graphic treatment of the names and will not represent finalized design concepts.

The revised headings and subheadings on the next page describe the section content more accurately and make it easier for readers to find details they need.

REVISION

ESTABLISHING A NEW CORPORATE IDENTITY

Background

Milburn and Associates plans to develop a new identity, including a new name and new graphics. At the company, you recognize a need for broader public recognition and an image that is appropriate for the 21st century. At Paradigm, we are ready to help with that process.

Milburn and Associates started refining and producing paper in 1990; although you have continued to introduce new products, you have made few changes to your image. As a result of information gleaned from customer surveys and opinions voiced by members of the Board of Directors, management has decided to modify the way the company presents itself to the public.

Our Approach

Interview Key Managers and Customers

To begin our search for a new identity for Milburn and Associates, Paradigm will interview six managers responsible for developing, managing, and marketing the company's paper products. We also plan to interview selected customers to attain a more in-depth understanding of your long-term business objectives, target markets, communications channels, desired image, and identity.

Review Company Records

We will review any existing research, corporate planning documents, and statements of corporate objectives that might help us understand your identity needs. While we do not need exhaustive information, we do want a clear understanding of major corporate issues and directions. We will also review any names you have previously developed and considered.

Present Preliminary List of Names and Design Concepts

Based on the results of the interviews and research, our team will prepare a short list of finalist names. Criteria for selecting names will include how effectively the names meet the communication objectives, how memorable the names are, whether they are easy to pronounce, their graphics potential, and their potential advertising impact.

The design team will then investigate design concepts for each of the name candidates. This design step will show the potential for graphic treatment of the names and will not represent finalized design concepts.

EXERCISE

· · · · · · · ·

Think of a long document you need to outline. List your sections, group them, and write out summary statements in the space below.

ACTIVITY:
A MILLION-DOLLAR PROPOSAL
· ·

Look back at the report outline that you began on page 20 when you imagined that your organization was likely to make a perfect resource available to you or your department. Follow these three steps to develop your outline into **A PROPOSAL FOR YOU TO RECEIVE THIS RESOURCE.**

1. Picture a resource that would be wonderful to have, but relatively plausible. You might visualize a fleet of minivans or state-of-the-art technology, or a thousand dollars, one million dollars, or more.

2. Use the space below to expand your report outline. For every heading that you identified on page 20 to report on current situations, add **A SECOND NEW HEADING** here:

   - How things are in your department now

   - **HOW MUCH BETTER THINGS WOULD BECOME, WITH THE NEW RESOURCE**

3. Decide what you'll include in the body of the document, what you'll eliminate, and what you'll put in an appendix. (The next chapter will give you a chance to expand this **PROPOSAL** outline into a **PROCEDURE** for how you *will* use the resource, after writing a successful proposal.)

3   DRAFT YOUR DOCUMENT

Your completed outline will make writing easier by providing a logical structure for your entire document. You've already accomplished these tasks:

- Decided what information to include

- Organized that information into sections and subsections

- Written headings and subheadings

- Summarized the key information

Writing the first draft is now a matter of filling in the details, section by section. As you write, you'll use your summary statements to help readers focus on key information and follow your facts and ideas. You'll also determine when to present information in the narrative form of sentences and paragraphs and when to use lists and charts.

The lesson will prepare you to take these actions:

- Follow your section outlines to draft your document

- Develop useful lists, charts, and visuals

- Draft document introductions

- Draft document summaries

- Compose key sentences that express your most important messages

Follow your section outlines to begin writing

You'll draft the body of your document one section at a time. As you draft sections, keep the following points in mind:

- **IDENTIFY THE MOST EFFECTIVE WAY TO PRESENT SPECIFIC INFORMATION.** Paragraph-based narratives are best for some information, such as explanations. But other information is easier for readers to understand when it's broken down into a list. Lists are especially useful for information that falls naturally into a series of items that share a theme — a theme that you establish in the list's introductory statement.

LIST

We have done extensive research on three kinds of work stations. Each work station is easy to assemble, has a wide variety of components, and can be available by the time we need it. Here is the stations' availability for three collections:

- The Galway Green Collection can be delivered within 24 hours
- The Ultera Umbrian Collection is available within two weeks of the order
- The Chanticleer Collection is available within 21 days of the order

- **KEEP SENTENCES UNDER 30 WORDS, AND FOCUS ON ONE POINT.** The more technical and complex the information is, the shorter the sentence should be. Notice how much easier the revision is to read in this example.

ORIGINAL
(a single, extremely long sentence)

From January 1 to July 1, the number of accidents reported by branch offices remained fairly constant, with between 22–33 accidents reported each month, but by October 31, the accident rate had jumped from 22–33 per month to 47 accidents reported in October, 51 in November, and 43 in December, and this accident rate is not acceptable. **[59 words]**

REVISION
(three shorter sentences that are easier to read)

From January 1 to July 1, the number of accidents reported by branch offices remained fairly constant, with between 22–33 accidents reported each month. **[25 words]** By October 31, the accident rate had jumped to 47 accidents reported in October, 51 in November, and 43 in December. **[21 words]** This accident rate is not acceptable. **[6 words]**

- **KEEP PARAGRAPHS UNDER ABOUT EIGHT LINES LONG ON A PRINT-READY PAGE.** The paragraph's first sentence should focus readers on the main point. The details that follow should explain or expand on that main point.

SHORT PARAGRAPH

Sixteen single-family homes, roadways, and central community facilities will be constructed on the 22-acre site. The homes will be approximately 2,200 square feet on half-acre parcels. A single one-way road will provide access to the homes and common facilities. Common facilities will include a community house, swimming pool, tennis court, children's play area, and community garden.

Maintain the flow of ideas across sentences and paragraphs

Ideally, your ideas should flow from sentence to sentence and from paragraph to paragraph in a way that your readers can follow easily. Here's a three-step process to help sentences and paragraphs flow:

1. Identify an important word in the last sentence of one paragraph
2. Repeat that word in the first sentence of the next paragraph
3. Consider revising the part of speech (e.g., by changing a verb to a noun)

These two paragraphs illustrate that technique:

> ... The Evaluation Committee Chair will usually <u>communicate</u> this information while the full committee is in session.

> It may not be appropriate for this <u>communication</u> to occur during a formal session. In these cases, ...

In this example, the verb "communica<u>te</u>" is echoed by the following noun "communicat<u>ion</u>." This echo links the two paragraphs by repeating a familiar idea. The change from verb to noun also gives the reader a sense of logical progress.

This technique can also link two sentences. Seeing this kind of link can help it seem effortless to progress from one idea to the next throughout a document.

Develop useful lists, tables, charts, and visuals

How do you read long, multisection business documents? Chances are, you don't linger over the words the way you savor a finely written novel. Instead, you probably scan the document to pick out the main points and the details you need — aware of the clock and other tasks you need to perform in your workday.

Your goal as a writer is to help readers scan your document and find information as quickly as possible. Technical or complicated information can quickly become dull and intimidating when it's in paragraph form.

So look for opportunities to present information in lists, tables, charts, and visuals — rather than paragraphs. The paired examples below present the same information. But notice how much easier both revisions are to read. First, a table makes it easy to compare different procedures.

ORIGINAL PARAGRAPH

The checklist references all procedures found in the Training Manual that address orientation, employee benefits, discipline, and retirement packages. These procedures will be discussed in detail at the annual Personnel Managers' meeting in Phoenix. Please review these items so you will be ready with your questions and any recommendations. Items 74 through 83 address procedures that pertain to orientation of all new employees. Items 84 through 91 address requirements and processes to ensure that all employees understand their health insurance options. Items 92 through 94 address pre-retirement preparation. Pension plans and cafeteria benefits are addressed in items 95 through 101.

REVISED FORMAT WITH A TABLE

This checklist references all procedures found in the Training Manual that address orientation, employee benefits, discipline, and retirement packages. These procedures will be discussed in detail at the annual Personnel Managers' meeting in Phoenix. Please review them and bring your questions and recommendations to the meeting.

ITEMS	PROCEDURES
74–83	Orientation of new employees
84–91	Requirements and processes to ensure that all employees understand health insurance options
92–94	Pre-retirement preparation
95–101	Pension plans and cafeteria benefits

Now, notice how the bullets in the list revision below make it easy to identify the checklist's four topics and then identify how the procedures relate to each topic.

ORIGINAL PARAGRAPH

The checklist references all procedures found in the Training Manual that address orientation, employee benefits, discipline, and retirement packages. These procedures will be discussed in detail at the annual Personnel Managers' meeting in Phoenix. Please review these items so you will be ready with your questions and any recommendations. Items 74 through 83 address procedures that pertain to orientation of all new employees. Items 84 through 91 address requirements and processes to ensure that all employees understand their health insurance options. Items 92 through 94 address pre-retirement preparation. Pension plans and cafeteria benefits are addressed in items 95 through 101.

REVISED FORMAT WITH TWO LISTS

The checklist references four procedures found in the Training Manual:

- Orientation
- Employee benefits
- Discipline
- Retirement packages

These procedures will be discussed in detail at the annual Personnel Managers' meeting in Phoenix. Please review the following four sets of items so you will be ready with your questions and any recommendations:

- **Items 74 through 83** address orientation procedures for new employees
- **Items 84 through 91** address requirements and processes to ensure that all employees understand their health insurance options
- **Items 92 through 94** address pre-retirement preparation
- **Items 95 through 101** address pension plans and cafeteria benefits

The list revision takes up much more space — more than the table revision on the preceding page. But the added white space in the margins and between the paragraphs separates topics cleanly and also makes the information much easier to skim.

The list format also represents some very simple quantitative analytical work that the writers have undertaken. This analysis appears in the phrases "<u>four</u> procedures" and "the following <u>four</u> sets of items" in the two lists' introductory statements.

Identifying themes and grouping details together is a considerate form of quantitative analysis that makes intricate details easier to navigate through. See page 24 for a sidebar on counting your ideas.

Follow five guidelines to keep lists easy to read

You can use a list in business writing—and, often, you should use a list—whenever you present three or more related pieces of information. Lists are more effective than long paragraphs because they do three things:

- Communicate information quickly
- Save valuable writing time
- Reduce the chance of grammar and punctuation errors

To make sure your lists are easy to read, follow the five guidelines below. Full illustrations of each of these guidelines follow the list.

1. **INTRODUCE THE LIST.** Every list needs an introductory statement, if only a few words, that identifies the list's theme and puts its items in context. It usually looks better to leave a blank line or some paragraph spacing between the introductory statement and the first list item.

2. **MAKE SURE THAT ALL ITEMS BELONG ON THE LIST.** All items on the list should relate directly to the introductory statement's unifying theme.

3. **BE CONSISTENT WITH INITIAL CAPITALIZATION, SENTENCE STRUCTURE, AND END PUNCTUATION:**

   - If you capitalize the first word of one line, capitalize the first word in every line.

   - Items in any single list should all be complete sentences or all be sentence fragments. List items that are sentence fragments should not end in periods, and they do not have to begin with capital letters.

   - For lists of complete sentences, end punctuation (a period or question mark) is only necessary for each item if any one item contains more than one sentence (as this list item does). In any list of complete sentences, you must use end punctuation after *all* the list's items if even *one* list item has end punctuation.

4. **KEEP THE LIST PARALLEL IN FORM.** For example, if one item begins with an *-ing* word, then all items should begin with *-ing* words.

5. **ORGANIZE THE LIST FOR YOUR READERS.** Lists that include more than five or six items can be hard to follow. Make lists easier to read by organizing the items into main points and subpoints.

Here are examples to illustrate the five list guidelines you just read.

1. Introduce the list

A list should never stand alone: it needs an introductory statement. The first item in a list can't introduce the list itself.

WITHOUT AN INTRODUCTION
- We offer several thank-you gifts
- A 10% discount on purchases during May
- A discount coupon for the Milano Ristorante
- A complimentary bottle of our best olive oil

WITH AN INTRODUCTION

To express our appreciation for your business, we would like to offer you several thank-you gifts:

- A 10% discount on purchases during May
- A discount coupon for the Milano Ristorante
- A complimentary bottle of our best olive oil

Use lists as a team member or leader

Lists have a wide variety of professional applications, whether you're composing a document as the leader of a company or as a member of a small team — e.g.,

- Setting out a variety of tasks or goals for a strategic plan
- Breaking down intricate processes into tidy, chronological steps
- Breaking down intricate projects into clean phases with specific deadlines
- Identifying which tasks are completed and which tasks remain
- Itemizing a budget and allocating resources for different items

Lists aren't just for word processor documents. Look for ways to include lists in emails, business letters, and short professional documents you write, in addition to longer reports, proposals, and procedures. Whether you're a team leader, vice president, manager, or new hire, list formatting makes it easy for readers to literally follow your ideas.

2. Make sure that all items belong on the list and relate directly to the introductory statement

NOT ALL ITEMS RELATE TO THE INTRODUCTORY STATEMENT

To prepare the room for the training, please do the following:

- Set up the tables in a U shape
- Put two flipcharts in the front of the classroom
- Place the projector on the table in the corner
- <u>Design the training to include lots of exercises and opportunities to practice</u>

ALL ITEMS RELATE TO THE INTRODUCTORY STATEMENT

When the training is over, please do <u>four things</u>:

- Recycle used flipchart pages
- Turn off the projector and store it in the closet
- Put the tables and chairs back the way you found them
- Give the completed evaluations to Melissa

3. Be consistent with initial capitalization, sentences or sentence fragments, and end punctuation

Use end punctuation only when at least one item contains more than one complete sentence. In paragraphs, sentences' end punctuation (periods and question marks) tells readers when one sentence stops and another starts.

In lists, end punctuation is only necessary if an item contains more than one sentence. That's because the format of a list clearly shows where one item stops and another begins. It's not incorrect to use end punctuation for single sentences in a list. But if you use end punctuation for one item, you must use it for all items.

END PUNCTUATION UNNECESSARY

We are unable to meet the original deadline for the following reasons:

- Two team members resigned in October and we have been unable to replace them
- The client expanded the project scope
- Three weeks of heavy rain made it impossible to complete our investigation

END PUNCTUATION NECESSARY

Here is a summary of our findings:

- The costs of moving to a new location will be higher than we originally estimated.
- According to the most current figures, the total cost will exceed $150,000.
- If we delay the move for five years, we will need an additional 10,000 square feet of space.
- Only 30 percent of our employees say they would be willing to move out of <u>California. Over 60 percent, however, would be willing to consider a move within the northern area of the state.</u>

The following list is hard to read because its format is inconsistent.

INCONSISTENT

We are unable to meet the original deadline for the following reasons:

- Two team members resigned in October. We have been unable to replace them.
- expanded project scope
- Three weeks of heavy rain made it impossible to complete our investigation

The periods in the first item are inconsistent with the complete sentence in the third item, which has no period. The uncapitalized sentence fragment is distracting because its form is inconsistent with the other two items. As a general rule, start bulleted items with capital letters, which can help individual list items stand out.

Here's the same list in a consistent format.

CONSISTENT

We are unable to meet the original deadline for the following reasons:

- Two team members resigned in October, and we have been unable to re-place them
- The client expanded the project scope
- Three weeks of heavy rain made it impossible to complete our investigation

4. Make sure the items in the list maintain parallel form

The items in a list must be grammatically parallel — presented in the same form. For example, if one item begins with a verb, all the items must begin with verbs. If one item is a complete sentence, all the items must be complete sentences.

NOT PARALLEL

> The agenda for the March meeting includes the following:
>
> - <u>Discussion of</u> the new health plan, which will be available to all permanent full-time employees
> - <u>Whether to</u> revise the procedures manual
> - <u>Early</u>-retirement policy

PARALLEL

> At the March meeting, we will do the following:
>
> - <u>Discuss</u> the new health plan, which will be available to all permanent full-time employees
> - <u>Decide</u> whether to revise the procedures manual
> - <u>Draft</u> an early-retirement policy

5. Organize the list for your reader

As a general rule, keep lists short. There should be no more than five or six items per list. When long lists are necessary, reorganize them as two or more shorter lists under separate introductory statements.

It's fine for a new list theme to be as simple as this: "Here are two further points: • • ." You can also make long lists easier for your readers to scan by organizing the items into main points and subpoints.

TOO MANY ITEMS TO TAKE IN EASILY

Please supply the following for the conference that begins on October 22:

- 30 writing tablets for each meeting room
- Five laptops for the community room
- An overhead projector for each meeting room
- Coffee, tea, and pastry in the foyer each morning
- Four round tables for each meeting room
- A conference phone in the community room
- A basket of fruit for each table in the meeting rooms
- A registration table in the foyer

ITEMS ORGANIZED WITH SUBPOINTS

We will need a number of items for the conference that begins on October 22. Please supply the following in each meeting room:
- 30 writing tablets
- An overhead projector
- Four round tables
- A basket of fruit for each table

Please supply the following in the community room:
- Five laptops
- A conference phone

And please supply the following in the foyer:
- Coffee, tea, and pastry each morning
- A registration table

Try it:
· · · · · · · ·

Use the blank space below to rewrite this paragraph in list form. Remember to include an introductory statement that establishes the context and tells readers what the list is about. Make sure you present all items in parallel form.

> I reviewed the accountant's analysis and believe that there are several important points to keep in mind when deciding what rating to give the bank. First of all, the bank was recapitalized. Secondly, this infusion allowed the capital ratios to exceed the threshold; and thirdly, asset quality is weak but does not pose a significant threat to earnings or capital. Finally, there were significant losses this year, but indications are that the bank should show a profit next year.

Page 50 shows one revision strategy.

Cleanly outline a table of contents

Counting ideas is the key to successful outlining, and it's very similar to the analytical process you learned on page 24 and the list strategies you just learned. A table of contents outline is simply a list of your main ideas, organized with numbers and sublists.

Here's one standard list hierarchy with five levels of headings:

- A capitalized Roman numeral (e.g., "IV")
- A capitalized letter (e.g., "D")
- An Arabic numeral (e.g., "3")
- A lowercased letter (e.g., "c")
- A lowercased Roman numeral (e.g., "ii")

That hierarchy would make it possible to refer to section "IV.D.3.c.ii" and help a reader navigate to that section heading quickly. Another numbering system would assign the designation "4.4.3.3.2" to the same section.

The main point to remember is that an outline can't have just one subsection. If you divide any section, separate it into <u>two or more parts.</u>

INCORRECT:

I.   Purpose
II. Objectives
III. Roles:
    <u>A.   Who Will Participate</u>
IV. Further Considerations

CORRECT:

I.   Purpose
II. Objectives
III. Roles:
    <u>A.   Why Roles Are Separated</u>
    <u>B.   Who Will Participate</u>
IV. Further Considerations

REVISION
· · · · · · · ·

Here's one way to turn page 48's paragraph into a list. Your version may differ.

> I reviewed the accountant's analysis and believe there are several important points to keep in mind when deciding what rating to give the bank:
>
> - The bank was recapitalized
> - The infusion of capital allowed the capital ratios to exceed the threshold
> - Asset quality is weak but does not pose a significant threat to earnings or capital
> - There were significant losses this year, but indications are that the bank should show a profit next year

TRY IT AGAIN:
· · · · · · · · · · ·

Turn this paragraph into a list.

> One group of top prospects for our Premier accounts includes college graduates from 25–35 years old. People in this category tend to be single or single parents. They are likely to work in white-collar or service occupations. They tend to rent apartments in large cities. They have more debt than assets, their credit card ownership is about average, and they frequently purchase electronic equipment.

REVISION

Here's one way to revise this paragraph into a list. Your version may differ.

> One group of top prospects for our Premier accounts includes college graduates who are 25–35 years old. They tend to have the following characteristics:
>
> - Work in white-collar or service occupations
> - Be single or single parents
> - Rent apartments in large cities
> - Have more debt than assets
> - Have average credit card ownership
> - Frequently purchase electronic equipment

Use numbered lists for a sequence of steps

Numbered lists can be even more helpful than bulleted lists, but ask yourself whether bullets or numbers are more appropriate for information that you set in list format.

Do you have a sequence of chronological steps that the reader should follow in order? Then create a numbered list. Will you need to refer to individual list items later on in your document? Then a numbered list may give you a handy way to identify them—e.g., "When you address Point 4 above, be sure to …."

Finally, would your list mean exactly the same thing if you rearranged the order of the list items? Then use bullets. Numbers imply a chronological sequence, and a collection of bullets doesn't carry the logical meaning that a sequence of numerals does. Bullets help readers zero in faster on information in a list and hop more quickly from item to item.

Combine tables with lists

Sometimes the most effective way to present information is to combine a list with a table. Here's an example:

ORIGINAL

This project has three distinct stages. During Stage 1, which will take 4–5 weeks, we will meet with you and conduct preliminary research to identify the tasks that need to be performed. We will then prepare a detailed project plan and schedule. During Stage 2, which will take 5–6 months, we will carry out each task, meeting with you as needed to review the status of the project and make any necessary changes to the project scope. Stage 3 will take a final 3–4 weeks; during this time, we will evaluate our findings and submit a report detailing our recommendations.

REVISION

This project has three distinct stages:

STAGE 1: 4–5 weeks	• Meet with you and conduct preliminary research to identify tasks that need to be performed • Prepare a detailed project plan and schedule
STAGE 2: 5–6 months	• Carry out each task • Meet with you as needed to review project status • Make any necessary changes to project scope
STAGE 3: the final 3–4 weeks	• Evaluate findings • Submit a report detailing our recommendations

The table rows make it immediately, visually clear that the project has three distinct phases. The table formatting makes the length of each phase easy to find, and the list separates the tasks for each phase in a way that's much easier to skim than the dense original paragraph.

TRY IT:
· · · · · · · ·

Use the space below to revise this paragraph to become a list, table, or combination of the two.

There are many problems as a result of the lack of clear policies and procedures in the five underwriting areas (Appraisals, Loans, Feasibility Studies, Financial Data, and Loan Provisions). Appraisals are not being prepared according to guidelines. There are two problems with loans. They are in excess of the 100 percent loan-to-value limit prescribed by Federal regulations. They have also been funded before all required documentation has been received. In addition, there have been no feasibility studies, financial data is incomplete or missing and is unverified and/or unreviewed when submitted with loan applications, and finally, the loan provisions are inadequate to fund projects in their entirety.

Write your revision here.

REVISION

· · · · · · · · ·

Here's one possible revision:

The following problems are caused by the lack of clear policies and procedures in the underwriting areas:

UNDERWRITING AREA	PROBLEMS
Appraisals	Not being prepared according to guidelines
Loans	• In excess of the 100 percent loan-to-value limit prescribed by Federal regulations • Funded before all required documentation has been received
Feasibility studies	Not undertaken
Financial data	• Incomplete • Missing • Unverified and/or unreviewed when submitted with loan applications
Loan provisions	Inadequate to fund projects in their entirety

Use tables to make comparisons

Tables are especially useful to show comparisons. Notice that in the original example below, readers must figure out for themselves how the numbers relate to one another. The reader can see this relationship much more clearly in the introductory paragraph and table with its three revised columns.

ORIGINAL

Lack of access to health care has very serious consequences for our community. One critical measure of the inadequacy of health care is the State's infant mortality rate. In 2008, we were the 7th highest in terms of infant survival, while in 2012 our ranking declined to 14th place. Our rank in terms of the proportion of babies born with low birth weight dipped from 12th to 17th, and the rank in terms of pregnant women receiving prenatal care during the first trimester of pregnancy fell from 10th to 29th.

REVISION

Lack of access to health care has very serious consequences for our community. One critical measure of the inadequacy of health care is the State's infant mortality rate. Here is how the State ranked in 2008 compared with 2012:

CONSEQUENCES	RANKING	
	2008	2012
Infant survival	7th	14th
Proportion of babies born with low birth weight	12th	17th
Pregnant women receiving prenatal care during the first trimester	10th	29th

TRY IT:
· · · · · · · ·

Combine text with a new table to make it easier to understand the following information.

> In an effort to determine the cost benefits of using conservation techniques, the utility costs of two families with the same number and ages of residents were recorded. Houses were identical in square feet and building materials. One family was taught to use conservation techniques. The other family did not use conservation techniques. Costs were recorded for January and July. In January, without conservation, the cost for gas was $85.00 and $28.00 for electricity. For the family using conservation techniques, the cost was $62.00 for gas and $20.00 for electricity. In July, with no conservation, the gas cost was $43.00 and electricity cost, $27.00. Gas costs were $30.00 and electricity costs were $15.00 when using conservation techniques.

Use this space to develop your table.

REVISION

Your revision might resemble this paragraph and table.

In an effort to determine the cost benefits of using conservation techniques, the utility costs of two families with the same number and ages of residents were recorded. Houses were identical in square feet and building materials. One family was taught to use conservation techniques. The other family did not use conservation.

UTILITY COSTS WITH AND WITHOUT CONSERVATION

	GAS		ELECTRICITY	
	With conservation	**Without conservation**	**With conservation**	**Without conservation**
January	$62	$85	$20	$28
July	$30	$43	$15	$27

Make sure visual elements add value

These guidelines can help you use visual elements to illustrate or explain specific points:

- **MAKE SURE EVERY VISUAL SERVES A PURPOSE.** Don't include a visual just because you have it! Ask yourself whether it makes an idea more clear.

- **MAKE SURE DRAWINGS OR PHOTOGRAPHS ARE CLEAR.** Remember that the report may be photocopied, and some photographs are too dark or fuzzy to print clearly.

- **PLACE THE VISUAL WHERE THE READER NEEDS IT** — as close to the reference as possible. If you refer to a visual in the text, add something like, "See Photograph 3 below" or "See Graph 2 on page 32."

- **PROVIDE A CLEAR RELATIONSHIP BETWEEN THE VISUAL AND NEARBY INFORMATION.** For instance, you might write, "This photograph shows the difference between the architectural styles of the two buildings."

- **EXPLAIN COMPLICATED GRAPHS.** For instance, you might write, "As the graph on the facing page illustrates, productivity rose over 30 percent last quarter while absenteeism dropped 20 percent."

Use lists and visuals for procedures

Procedures require some careful planning. Take a look at these badly planned instructions for making soup, which are a form of procedure since they set out a series of steps to attain a specific goal — completed soup. Would you find this procedure easy to follow?

SOUP

The following process should be followed:

- 1 c. of red kidney beans and then 1 t salt and pepper added.

- A zucchini that has been chopped into medium-sized pieces, not peeled, and some chopped celery and green onions go in as well. A few leaves of chard are needed, which should be chopped, and chopped carrots.

- The other ingredients that should be included are: garlic, 1 T olive oil and 3 Tablespoons of butter if you wish.

- You will need a large cooking pot.

- The soup should be assembled by putting into the pot all of the ingredients mentioned above and also a can of solid packed tomatoes that have been mashed up. The kidney beans should also be mashed. Also some chopped parsley and celery.

- 2 ½ c of chicken broth also go into the pot.

- When the soup has been cooked, some red wine and ¼ c of pasta should be put into the pot with some basil.

- When the pasta is cooked, the soup can be served. Grated cheese on top.

- The numbers of servings are about six, serve with a salad and also French bread.

•

Do you find this procedure easy to read? Aside from uneven grammar, what breakdowns can you identify in the writer's effort to offer straightforward instructions that a reader would find crystal clear and easy to follow?

You'll be able to compare this procedure with a more carefully planned version below.

You have to plan, draft, and proof any set of procedures to convey authority and make them user friendly. The recipe above shows breakdowns at all three of those phases.

Carelessly written procedures confuse and frustrate readers. When you write carefully, instructions can sound so natural that it's as if they wrote themselves. A logical sequence of clear directions makes it more likely that readers will follow your guidelines and accept that you're a trustworthy authority on the processes you set out.

Here are the three phases to write procedures: planning, drafting, and proofing.

1. **Plan the procedure:**

    a. Formulate a clear objective, and brainstorm the steps readers should take to achieve that objective. If any visuals would help readers grasp any step of the procedure more clearly, then map out where you'll add an illustration for that step.

    b. Identify any group of steps that you can break down into smaller steps. (For instance, this planning phase is broken into three sub-steps, with this item representing Step 1b.)

    c. Assemble all the steps in order.

2. **Draft a list:**

    a. Assemble the main actions as a numbered or lettered list for a chronological sequence of steps. Create a sub-list for any step that breaks down into a series of smaller steps.

    b. Start a new list item for each action.

    c. Add a clearly labeled visual for any step that becomes more clear through illustration.

    d. Test the procedure to make sure the steps work.

3. **Proof the procedure:**

    a. Use parallel structure, active language, and consistent terminology (e.g., by not mixing "1 T olive oil" with "3 Tablespoons of butter").

    b. Be concise. Visuals can help make a procedure more brief because showing can be more direct than telling.

    c. Try to break down the list under subheadings if there are more than six items per section.

Numbered and lettered lists make chronological sequences of steps much easier to follow and cite. For example, writing "See Step 2d above" makes it possible for the reader to locate that step right away. Consider using the numeric system on page 49 for a procedure that's especially long.

Take another look at these poorly planned instructions for making soup.

SOUP

The following process should be followed:

- 1 c. of red kidney beans and then 1 t salt and pepper added.
- A zucchini that has been chopped into medium-sized pieces, not peeled, and some chopped celery and green onions go in as well. A few leaves of chard are needed, which should be chopped, and chopped carrots.
- The other ingredients that should be included are: garlic, 1 T olive oil and 3 Tablespoons of butter if you wish.
- You will need a large cooking pot.
- The soup should be assembled by putting into the pot all of the ingredients mentioned above and also a can of solid packed tomatoes that have been mashed up. The kidney beans should also be mashed. Also some chopped parsley and celery.
- 2½ c of chicken broth also go into the pot.
- When the soup has been cooked, some red wine and ¼ c of pasta should be put into the pot with some basil.
- When the pasta is cooked, the soup can be served. Grated cheese on top.
- The numbers of servings are about six, serve with a salad and also French bread.

•

How could the planning, drafting, and proofing phases improve this procedure? List two ways:

_____

_____

How many actions can you count in the recipe above? Make a list and put the actions in order here:

_____

_____

_____

_____

_____

_____

Here's a much clearer procedure for preparing soup. What steps can you identify from the preceding list that the author has applied?

MINESTRONE SOUP

Ingredients:

- 11 oz. can of red kidney beans
- 1 teaspoon salt
- ¼ teaspoon pepper
- 1 clove peeled and pressed garlic
- 1 tablespoon olive oil
- 1 zucchini
- 2 stalks celery
- 2 small carrots
- 2 green onions
- 4–5 leaves Swiss chard
- ¼ cup parsley
- 8 oz. can of solid-packed Italian tomatoes, mashed
- 2 ½ cups chicken broth (use vegetable broth for a vegetarian soup)
- ½ cup red wine
- ¼ cup elbow macaroni or small pasta shells

Directions:

1. Empty the kidney beans into the pot. Mash them, leaving about two-thirds of the beans whole.
2. Stir in salt, pepper, garlic, and oil.
3. Coarsely chop the zucchini, celery, carrots, onions, Swiss chard, and parsley and add them to the pot.
4. Stir in the canned tomatoes and broth.
5. Cover the pot and simmer the soup for 45–60 minutes.
6. Add the red wine and macaroni or pasta, and cook for another 10 minutes.

Optional: For a richer soup, add 3 tablespoons of butter.

•

Notice that the numbered list makes the chronological list easy to follow, while the parallel structure "Empty … Stir in … Coarsely chop" makes it easy to grasp each separate action.

Try It

Think of a professional process that you or your coworkers regularly carry out for your work. Formulate a list of actions and write them out here, following the procedural guidelines you've learned.

Use data-based visuals: charts

Charts make quantitative data clear, and they take different forms:

- Pie charts and ring charts (such as the first chart below) for percentages
- Line charts
- Area charts (such as the second chart below)
- Bar charts

Whatever form best suits your numeric data, keep your design simple. (The 2013–204 area chart below is almost as simple as a chart can get.) If you're concerned that a chart may deepen complexity without enhancing clarity, then either look for ways to simplify the chart or consider leaving it out.

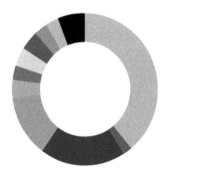

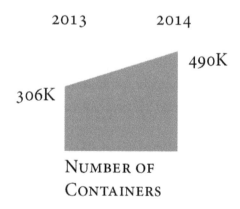

2013   2014

490K

306K

NUMBER OF
CONTAINERS

Draft an introduction

Complete the rest of your document before you write its introduction or any summary that you might need to include. You'll only know exactly what information to include in these sections when you've finished the rest of the document.

An introduction has two primary purposes: engaging your audience and setting the stage for the rest of your document. Introductions take different forms:

- An introduction can be an integral part of the document

- It can be a separate cover letter

- It can be an informal note

Introductions generally cover four functions:

- They inform readers of a document's topic and, sometimes, its purpose

- They briefly summarize any history readers will need to know as context to understand information in the following document

- They summarize key points such as findings, conclusions, and recommendations

- They summarize next steps, if the writer or reader will take further action

Keep your introductions short — say, 1.5 pages or less for most documents. Some introductions might be only a paragraph or two. Here are four general guidelines:

- As in the rest of the document, an introduction's paragraphs should be no more than 5–7 lines long.

- Leave out unnecessary information. For example, if readers need extensive background information, put it in a separate section or appendix and include only key points in the introduction.

- Include only main points from the document, leaving out inessential details. Remember that you've already identified your main points — they're the summary statements you developed in the outlining phase.

- It's sometimes appropriate for an introduction to include a brief list of participants in a project. But do not include such details as people's names, addresses, departments, or credentials. Instead, refer to a separate page where the information appears: "Four companies participated in this research. See page 7 for details."

Example

INTRODUCTION

Next summer the City of Laughing Hills will begin construction on a $3.1 million wastewater reclamation plant. The plant is intended to achieve two primary objectives:

- Treat wastewater flows to the levels set by the State Water Quality Control Agency

- Dispose effectively of treated effluent

The information contained in this report is summarized below.

Reasons for This Project

This project was undertaken for three reasons. The existing plant, constructed in 1982, fails to meet State standards. In 2007, partially treated sewage effluent was released into the system that serves as the source of irrigation water for the surrounding farmlands. Because the area is growing, the existing plant will be inadequate within five years.

Sources of Funding

This new facility will be funded through Farmers Home Administration grants and loans and special assessment bonds.

The Project Plan

The project will be conducted in three stages:

- Stage 1: Preliminary Planning, to begin June 15

- Stage 2: Facility Design, to begin October 15

- Stage 3: Facility Construction, to begin May 15

The Participants

Three companies will be involved in this project: Sorenson Associates, Leong and Hart, and Capwell Construction. See page 11 for details.

Use transition words to link your ideas

When full paragraphs of text are necessary, transition words and phrases help you relate a new topic to the previous one—smoothly connecting the separate parts of your writing. You may find transition words helpful when you string together your main points as you assemble and polish a document introduction.

Transitions are somewhat like the cartilage and tendons that hold your bones together: transitions form a connective tissue that links your ideas to one another. Transitions show readers how your ideas fit together; consequently, they help readers follow your points easily.

Here are some helpful transition words to use between sentences:

ADDITIONS
Also
And
As well as
Equally
For example
Furthermore
In addition
Moreover
Next
Now

CONTRASTS
Although
But
Despite
However
Nevertheless
Unless
Until

RESULT
Accordingly
As a consequence
As a result
For that reason
Of course
So that
Therefore
Thus

COMPARISONS
Equally
In the same way
Similarly

EMPHASIS
Again
Above all
As you asked
Certainly
Especially
Importantly
Indeed
In fact
In other words
In particular

SUMMARY
Finally
On the whole
To sum up

Draft a document summary

· ·

Introductions and summaries serve different purposes in long, multisection documents. The usual audience for an **INTRODUCTION** is people who will read all or some of the document that follows. The introduction's main purpose is to establish a context for what all readers will see.

On the other hand, your **SUMMARY** might be read by people who will never read the entire long document—or never even see it. It's important to craft summaries for these secondary readers. They need to see a concise overview of your most important message and the key facts you've included to inform or influence all your readers about that important message.

Write a summary only after you've developed your outline: this timing enables you to draw on the summary statements you drafted in Lesson 2. Here are some general guidelines for writing the summary for any multisection document:

- Keep the summary short. Between half a page and a full page is usually ideal; one-tenth of the entire document may be a reasonable maximum length.

- Remember that some readers may only read the summary. It should therefore be a compact statement of the document's most important points.

- Always state your most important message at the summary's beginning.

- Put the summary at the beginning of the document.

- Make sure that the summary covers all the main points and that they're in the same order as in the main document.

- Focus on the most important points. Remember that readers can always turn to the main document if they want or need more details.

The summaries of long documents, like their introductions, focus on the document's main points. You can therefore use the summary statements from your outline to develop your document summary.

Example

PROPOSAL SUMMARY

Westside Community Hospital Client Relations Program

During Phase 1, we will collect information about employees' interactions with clients and level of satisfaction with their working environment. Sources for information include firsthand observation; client and employee surveys; and private interviews with selected employees, clients, and managers; and focus groups.

At the end of Phase 1, we will summarize our findings and recommendations in a detailed report. The report will include a summary of what we learned, our analysis of the situation, and a plan to provide the hospital with a successful client relations program.

Depending on how quickly people respond to our requests for information and interviews, we can complete Phase 1 within four to six weeks of the start date. The not-to-exceed cost of this phase is $8,300.

Compose key sentences that express your most important messages

Finally, think of each paragraph's **KEY SENTENCE** as what you'd say if you had three seconds to get your most important message across before an elevator door closed. In each paragraph of a well-written long document, the sentence that carries the most important message should be so clear that the reader can identify it very easily, and it should usually begin a paragraph.

You've outlined your document sections, grouped your ideas into categories, and written a summary statement for the entire document. Your categories can now suggest key sentences to begin each paragraph of a section. Each key sentence should have three tasks:

- To introduce the paragraph's central topic

- To provide context to help readers follow your points

- To indicate which points are most important

You may be writing to pass on information to your readers — for instance, for a technical report. Informative key sentences should explain one new, smaller detail of your large, central document topic.

Or you may be writing primarily to persuade your readers — for instance, as part of a project proposal. In that case, a key sentence can expand your category heading into a statement that directly answers their question, "Why should we do what you want us to do — for instance, why should we pay for this additional service if we engage you for this project?"

ACTIVITY:
A MILLION-DOLLAR PROCEDURE
· ·

Look back at the proposal outline that you began on pages 20 and 34, when you imagined that your organization was likely to make a perfect resource available to you or your department. You've already outlined a **report** and a **proposal** on this topic. Follow the three steps below to revise your outline to become a **procedure** for your department's triumphant next steps.

1. Imagine that you have now received a wonderful, but relatively plausible, resource from your organization. (E.g., a fleet of minivans or state-of-the-art technology, or a thousand dollars, a million dollars, or more.) Imagine that your task now is to write to the decision makers who approved the resource transfer to explain, step by step, what you'll do next.

2. Use the space below to expand part of your proposal outline. Include this information:

    - **Your objective:** realizing the specific benefit(s) that the new resource will make possible

    - **Your procedure:** a step-by-step plan to attain this objective

3. Think about how you can use this chapter's guidelines for lists, charts, introductions, and summaries to outline a persuasive, effective procedure to improve your department. You'll probably find numbered lists especially helpful.

4   USE DYNAMIC LANGUAGE

Long, multisection documents are often difficult to read because the language is overly technical, wordy, passive, or pompous. To make sure readers can follow your points easily, use concise, active language and plain English. The more complex or technical your subject, the more important it is to use simple, clear language.

WHAT YOU'LL LEARN:

In this lesson you'll review the following aspects of dynamic professional language:

- Concise language
- Active language
- Problem-action-result (PAR) stories
- Plain English

OVERVIEW

The original paragraph below is so wordy, vague, passive, and imprecise that it's hard to tell what the writer meant to say. Notice how much easier it is to understand the revision.

ORIGINAL

The ways in which organizational information is communicated differs among those employees who work full-time and those employees who work part-time. Employees who work full-time tend to receive communication through formal channels such as newsletters, organizational social media, and meetings. Employees who work part-time, on the other hand, tend to receive the aforementioned information through the "grapevine," from their peers and people they work with.

REVISION

Full-time and part-time employees receive information about the organization differently. Full-time employees receive information through formal channels such as newsletters, organizational social media, and meetings, while part-time employees receive information from peers.

In this lesson, you'll learn methods that will help you keep your writing clear and easy to understand, no matter how complicated the information is. Then you'll be ready to apply what you learn by editing your own document. All the techniques in this lesson can help a team of writers share a unified, dynamic voice across document passages that they write separately.

Use concise language

Unnecessary words are an obstacle to clear writing. They clutter up your document, slow readers down, and make information hard to grasp.

CLUTTERED

The future site of the building is located at the corner of Fifth Street and Broadway.

CONCISE

The building site is at the corner of Fifth Street and Broadway.

CLUTTERED

The enclosed attachment to this letter is a sample of the Member Preferences Questionnaire which is used by the agency's Membership Department for the purpose of conducting an evaluation of preferences of our members.

CONCISE

We have attached a sample of the questionnaire the Membership Department uses to evaluate members' preferences.

Here are three ways to reduce clutter:

1. Use only one word for a one-word idea

2. Drop useless repetitions

3. Eliminate unnecessary *there are*, *who*, *that*, and *which* clauses

1. Use only one word for a one-word idea

CLUTTERED

All materials we purchase with these funds will be American made, and procurements will be done through an open and competitive process.

CONCISE

All materials we purchase with these funds will be American made, and we will procure them through an open and competitive process.

CLUTTERED

If the EC member has any clarification questions for the offerors, they must be communicated in writing to the Evaluation Leader.

CONCISE

EC members must write to the Evaluation Leader with any clarification questions for the offerors.

2. Drop useless repetition

CLUTTERED

The only <u>recorded conversations</u> about the property ownership dispute <u>recorded in the plaintiff's office</u> were two <u>conversations recorded at the plaintiff's facility</u> nearly four months after the dispute regarding property ownership began.

CONCISE

The only two recorded conversations about the property ownership dispute took place in the plaintiff's office, nearly four months after the dispute began.

The following two-word phrases feature unnecessary words.

USELESS REPETITIONS

• alternative choices	=	alternatives
• basic fundamental facts	=	fundamental facts
• end result	=	results
• past experience	=	experience
• advance warning	=	warning
• equally as effective as	=	equally effective
• desirable benefits	=	benefits
• serious crisis	=	crisis
• final outcome	=	outcome
• future plans	=	plans
• the equal halves	=	the halves
• regular weekly reports	=	weekly reports

3. Eliminate unnecessary
there are, *who*, *that*, and *which* clauses

CLUTTERED

There are three benefits which will result from reorganizing the HR Department.

CONCISE

Reorganizing the HR Department will yield three benefits.

CLUTTERED

The study that is being conducted separately by Morris Associates will be complete by September.

CONCISE

The separate Morris Associates study will be complete by September.

TRY IT:

· · · · · · ·

Revise these sentences to eliminate unnecessary words.

1. This report describes the process by which the manufacturing process is to be made more efficient than it currently is.

2. An analysis of the demographics reveals that 30 percent of our customers are located in only five major cities, and that three of those cities are located in the western half of the country.

3. In order to eliminate possible confusion in the future, we are requesting that all documents that are necessary to complete the application process be directed to Smit and Co.

4. It would be beneficial to us to have the comments returned to us as soon as it is possible for you to do so.

5. There are three factors that must be taken into consideration by your team.

6. Data collected to date is indicative of very low levels of pesticides in the ground water, according to the results of our investigation at this time.

7. We will provide additional details on compliance guidelines and incorporate the compliance guidelines into the final project report, which is due to be completed and submitted by October 1.

8. English and Spanish are the languages spoken by the workers, and the training should be documented in both of these languages.

9. It is our recommendation that you proceed to conduct a thorough review of the loans that were made during the period beginning on January 1 and ending on June 30 of this year.

ANSWERS

· · · · · · · · ·

The revisions follow the original sentences after each number below.

1.

This report describes the process by which the manufacturing process is to be made more efficient than it currently is.

This report describes how we can make the manufacturing process more efficient.

2.

An analysis of the demographics reveals that 30 percent of our customers are located in only five major cities, and that three of those cities are located in the western half of the country.

An analysis of the demographics reveals that 30 percent of our customers are in only five major cities, three of which are in the western half of the country.

3.

In order to eliminate possible confusion in the future, we are requesting that all documents that are necessary to complete the application process be directed to Smit and Co.

A number of documents are needed to complete the application process. To eliminate possible confusion, please direct them all to Smit and Co.

4.

It would be beneficial to us to have the comments returned to us as soon as it is possible for you to do so.

Please return the comments as soon as possible.

5.

There are three factors that must be taken into consideration by your team.

Your team must consider three factors.

6.

Data collected to date is indicative of very low levels of pesticides in the ground water, according to the results of our investigation at this time.

Our investigation indicates very low levels of pesticides in the ground water.

7.

We will provide additional details on compliance guidelines and incorporate the compliance guidelines into the final project report, which is due to be completed and submitted by October 1.

We will provide additional details on compliance guidelines and incorporate them into the final project report, which is due on October 1.

8.

English and Spanish are the languages spoken by the workers, and the training should be documented in both of these languages.

The workers speak English and Spanish, and the training should be documented in both languages.

9.

It is our recommendation that you proceed to conduct a thorough review of the loans that were made during the period beginning on January 1 and ending on June 30 of this year.

We recommend that you thoroughly review the loans made this year between January 1 and June 30.

Use active language

Passive language is fine in some situations:

- **WHEN IT DOESN'T MATTER WHO TOOK ACTION** (e.g., who performed the demolition work in this sentence: "Before we purchased the site, one storage shed was partially demolished")

- **WHEN THE READERS KNOW WHO TOOK THE ACTION, AND THE FOCUS SHOULD BE ON THE ACTION ITSELF** (e.g., a report might name the members of a scientific team, explain that they measured soil samples, and then include the passive statement "Samples were obtained from five sites across the region")

However, it's best to use active language whenever you can: it keeps your writing clear, dynamic, and concise. Active language focuses readers' attention and communicates directly and powerfully. Passive language can weaken writing and confuse readers; it can also make sentences longer.

PASSIVE

The decision was made by the company that the largest processing plant would be renovated in three years.

ACTIVE

The company **decided to renovate** the largest processing plant in three years.

Here are three guidelines for using active language:

1. Don't just say what was done: say who did something

2. Use strong verbs instead of colorless verbs such as *is*, *was*, *does*, and *has* (e.g., "The managers decided" instead of "it was decided by the managers")

3. Give clear instructions instead of hinting at actions (e.g., "Lift the lid of the scanner" instead of "The lid of the scanner is then to be lifted")

Active language can help a team achieve a consistent tone across document sections that different people draft. If everyone follows the guidelines in this lesson, these shared writing approaches can help even out the writing style and give the document a more consistent and more dynamic feel.

1. Don't just say what was done: say who did something

ACTOR LEFT OUT [passive]

A new procedure has been designed to process unpaid bills.

ACTOR SPECIFIED [active]

Accounting has designed a new procedure to process unpaid bills.

ACTOR LEFT OUT [passive]

Your submittal has been reviewed for compliance with Specification 12.

ACTOR SPECIFIED [active]

We have reviewed your submittal for compliance with Specification 12.

2. Use strong verbs instead of colorless verbs such as *is*, *was*, *does*, and *has*

COLORLESS VERB [passive]

A definition of the term *drinking water* is provided in the Act.

STRONG VERB [active]

The Act defines the term *drinking water*.

COLORLESS VERB [passive]

A survey was taken of employees to determine the benefits package that is preferred by them.

STRONG VERB [active]

Personnel surveyed employees to determine which benefits package they prefer.

3. Give clear instructions
instead of hinting at actions

INDIRECT [passive]

The sluice gate must <u>be opened</u> before the containers <u>are unloaded</u>.

DIRECT [active]

<u>Open</u> the sluice gate before <u>you unload</u> the containers.

INDIRECT [passive]

The black knob should <u>be turned</u> carefully to the right until the red light can <u>be seen</u> on the console.

DIRECT [active]

<u>Carefully turn</u> the black knob to the right until <u>you see</u> the red light on the console.

TRY IT:

Revise the passive language in these sentences to become active and direct. If necessary, use your imagination to supply an actor.

PASSIVE

The proposal <u>was completed</u> on time.

ACTIVE

<u>Sue's team completed</u> the proposal on time.

1. Arrangements for the exhibit were handled by Meeting Planners.

2. Included in this report are the results of our investigation.

3. It is believed that little relevant data would be provided by further testing.

4. The proposed location of the new manufacturing facility will be discussed with the executive staff before any action is taken.

5. After all research results have been received, an assessment will be made of the full extent of the problem, and recommendations will be presented for Phases 4 and 5.

6. A client satisfaction survey was conducted by the Marketing Director to confirm information obtained by her during informal conversations with clients.

7. Distribution of guidelines for emergency room visits is the sole responsibility of the health maintenance organization.

8. The paid invoices should be filed by company name in the blue cabinet, and the accounts should then be updated on the computer.

ANSWERS
· · · · · · · · ·

Each number includes the original sentence and a revised line below it.

1.

Arrangements for the exhibit were handled by Meeting Planners.

<u>Meeting Planners handled</u> arrangements for the exhibition.

2.

Included in this report are the results of our investigation.

<u>This report includes</u> the results of our investigation.

3.

It is believed that little relevant data would be provided by further testing.

<u>We believe</u> that <u>further testing would provide</u> little relevant data.

4.

The proposed location of the new manufacturing facility will be discussed with the executive staff before any action is taken.

<u>We will discuss</u> the proposed location of the new manufacturing facility with the executive staff before <u>we take</u> any action.

5.

After all research results have been received, an assessment will be made of the full extent of the problem, and recommendations will be presented for Phases 4 and 5.

After <u>we have received</u> all research results, <u>we will assess</u> the extent of the problem and <u>present</u> recommendations for Phases 4 and 5.

6.

A client satisfaction survey was conducted by the Marketing Director to confirm information obtained by her during informal conversations with clients.

<u>The Marketing Director conducted</u> a client satisfaction survey to confirm information <u>she obtained</u> through informal conversations with clients.

7.

Distribution of guidelines for emergency room visits is the sole responsibility of the health maintenance organization.

<u>The health maintenance organization distributes</u> guidelines for emergency room visits. <u>This responsibility is</u> theirs alone.

8.

The paid invoices should be filed by company name in the blue cabinet, and the accounts should then be updated on the computer.

<u>File</u> paid invoices by company name in the blue cabinet and then <u>update</u> accounts on the computer. [The subject is an implied *you*, to address the reader.]

Use problem-action-result (PAR) stories to pitch your services

PAR stories are a formula to describe a **PROBLEM** you've faced in your work, an **ACTION** you took, and the beneficial **RESULTS** you achieved. This three-part chronological format is vivid and easy to follow, and it can help your readers see how your work could solve a problem that they face. The PAR format gives your readers a chronological structure:

- A problematic beginning
- A dynamic middle
- And a happy ending

PAR stories convey clear benefits to readers in a variety of documents. Here are some examples:

- A resume
- The About Us section of your website
- Or a high-stakes proposal that could bring in new work if it's persuasive

Remember that the *P* in *PAR story* stands for *"problems."* So any PAR story automatically demonstrates your problem-solving abilities. This storytelling format shows you solving problems, and it tells a success story where you're a professional hero — even if your professional heroics are relatively modest. "I saved everyone 30 minutes," or "the client thanked me afterward" are perfectly fine problems to include in a PAR story.

The problem in a PAR story can be as simple as "The client wanted to see something new ..." or "A customer was not satisfied...." Here's an example, with several underlined active verbs:

> The client company <u>needed</u> a new strategy to market its software. **[Problem]** Jill <u>spearheaded</u> an analysis of regional U.S. markets and <u>suggested</u> a three-phased marketing strategy. **[Action]** The resulting campaign <u>boosted</u> sales by 140 percent, so the company <u>duplicated</u> the strategy in its Australian and Canadian markets and <u>saw</u> similar sales boosts there. **[Result]**

PAR stories can help proposals explain how one employee's **PAST PERFORMANCE** demonstrates that she or he will be an ideal person to help a team achieve a specific objective. You can also cast PAR stories in **THE FUTURE** for a proposal, to predict successful problem solving:

> We recognise that your company wants three regional offices to improve their reputations for safety. **[Problem]** We are ready to customise our existing safety trainings to the unique challenges in each region. **[Action]** Our experience leads us to be confident that this customised approach will assure participants that we speak their language and feel engaged. Our post-testing will also give HR quantitative proof of the resulting expertise that participants gain. **[Result]**

Don't expect your readers to find it self-evident how your actions deliver beneficial results. You save readers time, write more clearly, and demonstrate well-earned self-respect when you spell out exactly how you or your team can deliver outcomes that others value.

PAR stories for team leaders, speakers, and managers

You may be familiar with PAR stories from resumes and cover letters, but they aren't just for landing a job. They're excellent tools in a variety of advanced professional settings:

- For teams and managers to add corroborating details to a proposal
- To bring a website's About Us section to life with one or more personal, compelling narratives
- For speakers to add to a presentation, to put a human face on business processes

Use plain English

Writers tend to complicate their writing by using these kinds of problematic language:

- Unnecessarily formal language that leaves readers guessing

- Jargon, including made-up words and phrases that some readers might not understand

Avoid unnecessarily formal language

Some language is more complicated or formal than it needs to be—forcing readers to mentally translate words and phrases into everyday language. Plain English communicates clearly and directly while still conveying a professional image.

TRY IT:

· · · · · · · ·

Fill in the blanks with words in plain English that convey the same meaning as the more complicated words in the column on the left. (The first line is filled in.)

INSTEAD OF ...	CONSIDER USING ...
prior to	before
magnitude	
facilitate	
aforementioned	
subsequent to	
terminate	
optimum	
initiate	
utilize	
pursuant to	
viable	
supplemental	
concurrence	
commence	

ANSWERS
· · · · · · · · ·

INSTEAD OF ...	CONSIDER USING ...
prior to	before
magnitude	size
facilitate	make easy, simplify
aforementioned	mentioned earlier
subsequent to	after, following
terminate	end
optimum	best
initiate	start, begin
utilize	use
pursuant to	in accordance with
viable	practical, workable
supplemental	extra, additional
concurrence	agreement
commence	begin, start

Avoid made-up language

People sometimes write in nonstandard ways on the grounds that creative language usage is necessary to describe the unique situations of their businesses. Here are some examples of made-up language.

- They asked him to <u>definitize</u> his plans.
- I took samples from the <u>sewered</u> area.
- Please contact <u>POE</u> as soon as possible.

Made-up language doesn't appear in the dictionary; readers may therefore have to guess what you meant with a made-up term, and their guesses may not match the meaning you had in mind. Your readers will find it easier to follow you if you stick with dictionary words and define any specialty terms you can't avoid.

It's especially important to avoid made-up language when a team writes a long document. If everyone aims for straightforward descriptions in plain English, it becomes much more easy to achieve a unified tone across document sections that different people drafted.

Spell out acronyms and define terms

Acronyms help you avoid spelling out long names repeatedly. But the first time you use an acronym, spell out what it stands for. Then repeat your explanation once in each long section in which you use the acronym.

In especially long documents, it's also helpful to redefine any rare terms you need to use. If a rare term appeared once in Chapter 1 with a definition and doesn't reappear until Chapter 4, then paste the same definition back into Chapter 4.

TRY IT:

· · · · · · · ·

Revise the following paragraphs so the language is concise, active, and clear. Use the space below or your computer to rewrite the paragraphs.

It is felt by all of us at Rothko and Associates that we are in the position of being able to deliver to you a data analysis system that will be more powerful than any other data analysis system available presently. We utilize state-of-the-art technology in order to maximize the accomplishment of your objectives. Our R&D Department is dedicated to the maintenance of our very unique position as leaders of our industry. We are enabled by the breadth and depth of the accomplishments and abilities of our large and experienced staff of experts to handle technical challenges of the most complex and complicated kinds.

To ensure that the process of development goes as smoothly as possible, a dedicated project team will be assembled by a project manager who is in possession of specific expertise for your project. Supporting the project manager will be a trained project analyst, whose responsibility will be to be of assistance with the myriad phases of development. A database specialist will be an essential element of the aforesaid team, charged with the responsibility of obtaining a representative sample as well as to assist you with an interpretation of the data. Other personnel will be brought in as required during the course of the project.

ANSWERS

Here's one revision. Yours may differ, but it should be clear, concise, and easy to read.

> Rothko Associates can deliver a data analysis system more powerful than any other system that is available now. We use state-of-the-art technology to help you meet your objectives. Our Research and Development Department is dedicated to maintaining our unique position as industry leaders. Our large, experienced staff provides the expertise our customers need to address the most complex technical challenges.
>
> To ensure that the development process goes smoothly, a project manager will assemble a team with specific expertise for your project. The team will include three kinds of specialist:
>
> - A project analyst to help with the development phases
> - A database specialist to obtain a representative sample and help you interpret the data
> - Other personnel as needed

ACTIVITY:
MILLION-DOLLAR LANGUAGE

Look back at the three outlines that you wrote for Lessons 1 through 3, when you imagined that your organization would make a perfect resource available to you or your department.

1. Think of the three outlines you wrote earlier, and choose one of them to expand:

   - The **REPORT** you outlined on page 20 to give readers important information

   - The **PROPOSAL** you outlined on page 34 to persuade readers to take action

   - The **PROCEDURE** you outlined on page 70 to set out a step-by-step plan to attain a specific objective

2. Use the techniques from this lesson to draft a short section from one of these three outlines. You could use dynamic language for this draft by writing a problem-action-result story. Or you could simply use concise, active, plain English that your readers will find easy to follow.

Congratulations: you've completed this workbook!

About Write It Well

Write It Well began in 1979 as Advanced Communication Designs, Inc. We're a firm of trainers and professional-development consultants who help people in business communicate more efficiently and effectively. We offer training, coaching, and writing and editing services.

We provide practical, job-relevant information, techniques, and strategies that readers and training participants can apply right away to the documents they produce and presentations they deliver for their jobs. Many individuals and organizations use our books and training programs — including teams, training specialists, instructors in corporations and businesses of all sizes, nonprofit organizations, government agencies, and colleges and universities.

The Write It Well Series on Business Communication includes the self-paced training courses *Professional Writing Skills*; *Effective Email: Concise, Clear Writing to Advance Your Business Needs*; *Land the Job: Writing Effective Resumes and Cover Letters*; *Develop and Deliver Effective Presentations*; *Reports, Proposals, and Procedures*; and *Writing Performance Reviews*. Visit writeitwell.com for more information about our company and detailed descriptions of our publications and services.

About the author

Natasha Terk leads Write It Well's business operations and strategy. She holds master's degrees from the University of San Francisco and the University of Manchester, UK. She has served as a program officer at the Packard Foundation, a management consultant with La Piana Consulting, and a board member for the Ronald McDonald House of San Francisco.

Natasha has taught business writing at the University of California, Berkeley and has been a consultant for Berkeley's Haas School of Business. She leads onsite and online webinars and workshops for clients including Dreyer's Grand Ice Cream, Hewlett-Packard, Visa, IKEA, Bank of America, and the City of Palo Alto. She gives keynote speeches and presentations on business communications at seminars and large conferences.

Lightning Source UK Ltd.
Milton Keynes UK
UKHW030625150519
342714UK00007B/973/P